Dash to the Log Pile

By Sally Cowan

Clove and Pete are in the den.

Mum is not at home.

Pete pokes his nose out.

The log pile is up the slope at Scamp's home.

It is not safe!

Dogs can chase little kits!

The skunk kits dash up the slope and dive onto the log pile!

Scamp wakes up.

He can see two small black and white shapes.

Mum gets home.
She can use her nose
to smell the kits' tracks.

Mum lopes up the slope
to the log pile.

The kits hide.

"Get away from my kits!"
Mum yells at Scamp.

Scamp sees Mum's
black and white stripes.

She will strike him with mist!

He runs away to hide.

“Time to go home, kits!” calls Mum, with a smile.

CHECKING FOR MEANING

1. Which skunk kit suggests they should go out? *(Literal)*
2. What made the log pile unsafe? *(Literal)*
3. Do you think Mum was angry with Scamp? Why? *(Inferential)*

EXTENDING VOCABULARY

safe	What does it mean to be safe? What are some things that help keep you safe?
cute	What other animals do you think are cute? What makes an animal cute?
stripes	Read the word *stripes*. What are the sounds in this word? What do stripes look like? Where else might you see stripes?

MOVING BEYOND THE TEXT

1. Skunks spray a stinky mist to protect themselves. Why would that make other animals stay away from them?
2. How do other animals protect themselves?
3. What other animals can you think of that live in a den? Do you think a den is a good home for an animal? Why?
4. Mum used her sense of smell to find the kits. Why is sense of smell important? What are the other four senses?

TIME TO WRITE

Imagine you are Scamp. Write the story from his point of view.

PRACTICE WORDS